Ten Poems
of the Soil

*to Tony & Liz
in Cambridge
before Henry
& Auguste
22*

ex li

Candlestick Press

Published by:

Candlestick Press,
Diversity House, 72 Nottingham Road, Arnold, Nottingham NG5 6LF
www.candlestickpress.co.uk

Design and typesetting by Craig Twigg

Printed by Ratcliff & Roper Print Group, Nottinghamshire, UK

Selection and Introduction © Di Slaney, 2022

Cover illustration © Sara Boccaccini Meadows, 2022
www.boccaccinimeadows.com

Candlestick Press monogram © Barbara Shaw, 2008

Donation to Soil Association
www.soilassociation.org

ISBN 978 1 913627 04 1

Acknowledgements

The poems in this pamphlet are reprinted from the following books, all by
permission of the publishers listed unless stated otherwise. Every effort has been
made to trace the copyright holders of the poems published in this book. The
editor and publisher apologise if any material has been included without
permission or without the appropriate acknowledgement, and would be glad to be
told of anyone who has not been consulted.

Thanks are due to all the copyright holders cited below for their kind permission:

Margaret Atwood, *Selected Poems 2: 1976-1986: vol. 2* (Mariner Press, 1987) by
permission of Curtis Brown, Inc. Carl Dennis, *Poetry* (May 2003) by kind
permission of The Poetry Foundation. Jacqueline Gabbitas, first published by
Stonewood Press, by kind permission of the poet. Adam Horovitz, *The Soil Never
Sleeps: Poetry from a Year on Four British Farms,* Ed. 1 (Palewell Press 2018).
Katie Hourigan, first published in *Spelt,* by kind permission of the poet. Yusef
Komunyakaa, *Pleasure Dome: New and Collected Poems* (Wesleyan University
Press, 2004). Used by permission. PK Page, *The Hidden Room* - in two volumes
(Porcupine's Quill, 1997). Ruth Pitter, *Collected Poems* (Enitharmon Press,
1990). George Szirtes, *New & Collected Poems* (Bloodaxe Books, 2008)
www.bloodaxebooks.com

All permissions cleared courtesy of Suzanne Fairless-Aitken
c/o Swift Permissions swiftpermissions@gmail.com

Where poets are no longer living, their dates are given.

Contents   Page

Introduction

I'm lucky to own a field which not so long ago was an unloved scrubby bit of land, more weeds and holes than anything else, but is now home to over 180 different animals plus abundant wildlife, trees and hedges. None of this richness of flora and fauna would have been possible without soil – the "good soil" that Verne Bright talks about so beautifully in his poem of the same name. And it is only good soil because of the creatures and plants that live in and on it, replenishment being inextricably linked to what goes on above and below ground.

The poems in this mini-anthology bring to life those terranean activities in all their diversity. We have worms busy at their vitally important – if unacknowledged – endeavours in Carl Dennis's poem, and a diligent excavating mole who "opens his own doors" according to PK Page. Mushrooms are the inspiration for an elegiac poem by Margaret Atwood, who describes how they "ooze up through the earth", transforming "flesh into earth into flesh".

Meanwhile people are hard at work too, following a "horse-drawn plow / that opened up the soil" to bank potatoes in Yusef Komunyakaa's poem and to "dig and double-dig the clay" as Ruth Pitter shows how effort equals reward for 'The Diehards'. Katie Hourigan's poem 'Jenny' is a close-up of someone's very personal relationship with soil, meaning so much more than simply raising plants, echoing George Szirtes describing how soil "creeps under your skin" until "suddenly a dull music has begun".

The working of the land – by humans and other creatures – clearly has great benefits for all living things. But then there's just the sheer beauty of nature at work – Jacqueline Gabbitas musically evokes how 'Ground breaks for the coming of spring', and Adam Horovitz tells us that "The soil never sleeps", providing "a rooftop on another world." I hope you enjoy these glimpses of that other world, standing on a piece of earth that's special to you.

Di Slaney

The Soil Never Sleeps

The soil never sleeps.
In its voids, gas and waters gather,
waiting for thirsty roots to crawl
down motorway tunnels dug by worms.
For the spade. The plough.
The massage-press of hooves.
For the rain to run through its seams
and seeds to push up to the light.

The soil never sleeps.
It banks lives
in its soufflé stomach,
connects them to everything.
Even the dirt beneath fingernails,
the dirt caught in a mole's coat, sings
with a million microbes to the gram
of connections, growth.

The soil never sleeps.
Never slips into ideology or nostalgia.
It is place and purpose,
the perfection of decay.
A story that shifts
from mouth to mouth.
A crucible for rebirth.
A rooftop on another world.

Adam Horovitz

Good Soil

This is good soil: begetter of tall grain,
Blackberry, sloe, rough bramble from the rock,
Barley and stinging rye, cool mullein, dock,
Heartsease and cornflower under the sounding rain;
The sensitive corn, root-tip and sworded leaf,
In misty shafts of green leaning to the drip
Of gold rain-music slow and sweet, the grip
Of bean-vine over its heart; the gorgeous brief
Miracle of grass...
                    This is good soil:
Out of this earth life blooms a day, a year;
Into this earth life goes – the dark loam, dear
Cozener of flesh! the breaker of long toil!
Meal of marl, warm shelly sand, and stone:
This is good soil... to cover the taken bone.

Verne Bright (1893 – 1977)

Banking Potatoes

Daddy would drop purple-veined vines
Along rows of dark loam
& I'd march behind him
Like a peg-legged soldier,
Pushing down the stick
With a V cut into its tip.

Three weeks before the first frost
I'd follow his horse-drawn plow
That opened up the soil & left
Sweet potatoes sticky with sap,
Like flesh-colored stones along a riverbed
Or diminished souls beside a mass grave.

They lay all day under the sun's
Invisible weight, & by twilight
We'd bury them under pine needles
& then shovel in two feet of dirt.
Nighthawks scalloped the sweaty air,
Their wings spread wide

As plowshares. But soon the wind
Knocked on doors & windows
Like a frightened stranger,
& by mid-winter we had tunneled
Back into the tomb of straw,
Unable to divide love from hunger.

Yusef Komunyakaa

The Diehards

We go, in winter's biting wind,
On many a short-lived winter day,
With aching back but willing mind
To dig and double-dig the clay.

All in November's soaking mist
We stand and prune the naked tree,
While all our love and interest
Seem quenched in blue-nosed misery.

We go in withering July
To ply the hard incessant hoe;
Panting beneath the brazen sky
We sweat and grumble, but we go.

We go to plead with grudging men,
And think it is a bit of luck
When we can wangle now and then
A load or two of farmyard muck.

What do we look for as reward?
Some little sounds, and scents, and scenes:
A small hand darting strawberry-ward,
A woman's apron full of greens.

A busy neighbour, forced to stay
By sight and smell of wallflower-bed;
The plum-trees on an autumn day,
Yellow, and violet, and red.

Tired people sitting on the grass,
Lulled by the bee, drugged by the rose,
While all the little winds that pass
Tell them the honeysuckle blows.

The sense that we have brought to birth
Out of the cold and heavy soil,
These blessed fruits and flowers of earth
Is large reward for all our toil.

Ruth Pitter (1897 – 1992)

The Mole

The mole goes down the slow dark personal passage –
a haberdasher's sample of wet velvet moving
on fine feet through an earth that only
the gardener and the excavator know.

The mole is a specialist and truly
opens his own doors; digs as he needs them
his tubular alleyways; and all his hills
are mountains left behind him.

PK Page (1916 – 2010)

Ground breaks for the coming of spring

My eyes are blind.
Everything, all beasts and birds,
all things that prey, are preyed on,
know how blind my eyes are, how
I find sun and sky by inheritance.
This they knew when they came to be.

I am passing through earth, passing
the souls of animals who nod
when my eyes (like a newborn worm)
seek them out for guidance.

My world has been glacial
and all I had was the roar of god,
then the small click of ice breaking.
My world has been burning,
and all I had was heat and carbon:
light surrounding. Until the ash.
I have known all states of things.

Each year I break through blind
to open my eyes for the sun, sky,
for the bridge of leaves above trees;
the creatures sleeping newly beneath them.

Jacqueline Gabbitaş

Worms

Aren't you glad at least that the earthworms
Under the grass are ignorant, as they eat the earth,
Of the good they confer on us, that their silence
Isn't a silent reproof for our bad manners,
Our never casting earthward a crumb of thanks
For their keeping the soil from packing so tight
That no root, however determined, could pierce it?

Imagine if they suspected how much we owe them,
How the weight of our debt would crush us
Even if they enjoyed keeping the grass alive,
The garden flowers and vegetables, the clover,
And wanted nothing that we could give them,
Not even the merest nod of acknowledgment.
A debt to angels would be easy in comparison,
Bright, weightless creatures of cloud, who serve
An even brighter and lighter master.

Lucky for us they don't know what they're doing,
These puny anonymous creatures of dark and damp
Who eat simply to live, with no more sense of mission
Than nature feels in providing for our survival.
Better save our gratitude for a friend
Who gives us more than we can give in return
And never hints she's waiting for reciprocity.

"If I had a nickel, I'd give it to you,"
The lover says, who, having nothing available
In the solid, indicative world, scrapes up
A coin or two in the world of the subjunctive.
"A nickel with a hole drilled in the top
So you can fasten it to your bracelet, a charm
To protect you against your enemies."

For his sake, she'd wear it, not for her own,
So he might believe she's safe as she saunters
Home across the field at night, the moon above her,
Below her the loam, compressed by the soles of her loafers,
And the tunneling earthworms, tireless, silent,
As they persist, oblivious, in their service.

Carl Dennis

Mushrooms

i

In this moist season,
mist on the lake and thunder
afternoons in the distance

they ooze up through the earth
during the night,
like bubbles, like tiny
bright red balloons
filling with water;
a sound below sound, the thumbs of rubber
gloves turned softly inside out.

In the mornings, there is the leaf mold
starred with nipples,
with cool white fishgills,
leathery purple brains,
fist-sized suns dulled to the color of embers,
poisonous moons, pale yellow.

ii

Where do they come from?

For each thunderstorm that travels
overhead there's another storm
that moves parallel in the ground.
Struck lightning is where they meet.

Underfoot there's a cloud of rootlets,
shed hairs or a bundle of loose threads
blown slowly through the midsoil.
These are their flowers, these fingers
reaching through darkness to the sky,
these eyeblinks
that burst and powder the air with spores.

iii

They feed in shade, on halfleaves
as they return to water,
on slowly melting logs,
deadwood. They glow
in the dark sometimes. They taste
of rotten meat or cloves
or cooking steak or bruised
lips or new snow.

iv

It isn't only
for food I hunt them
but for the hunt and because
they smell of death and the waxy
skins of the newborn,
flesh into earth into flesh.

Here is the handful
of shadow I have brought back to you:
this decay, this hope, this mouth-
ful of dirt, this poetry.

Margaret Atwood

Jenny

She pulls things from the earth
with bare hands, clipped fingernails crusted,
compact with the black.
Roll the stem, between this finger and that,
then ease; out of that musty damp
the bulk of root, to straggling tip.
Japanese radish, long as thumbs, lobster pink with
peppered, brittle flesh;
beet that bleed into scored wood
stain fingertips in violent ink –
she shakes all this life in her hands,
sieves the clotted soil and breadcrumbs dirt.
Plucking at broad beans, freeing
full fat pods from strained seams,
peering at pale bright flesh, their bitter caps
she'll not look up.
'There's something pressing in my head.'
She pulls things from the earth.

Katie Hourigan

Soil

What colour would you call that now? That brown
which is not precisely the colour of excrement
or suede?
The depth has you hooked. Has it a scent
of its own, a peculiar adhesiveness? Is it weighed,
borne down

by its own weight? It creeps under your skin
like a landscape that's a mood, or a thought
in mid-birth,
and suddenly a dull music has begun. You're caught
by your heels in that grudging lyrical earth,
a violin

scraped and scratched, and there is nowhere to go
but home, which is nowhere to be found
and yet
is here, unlost, solid, the very ground
on which you stand but cannot visit
or know.

George Szirtes

Afterword

Dear Friends,

We hope you enjoyed this collection of poems as much as we did.

It's a joy to share in the wonders of the natural world, and this reminds us more than ever of the importance of protecting the future of our planet by working with nature.

Today we face crises in nature, our climate and health, but we see a future where that can be different.

A world with good health, in balance with nature and a safe climate, starts by looking after our soil.

Just as the global crises are connected, so are the solutions, and soil is the greatest connector of all. It touches almost every element of our lives. No matter who we are, it is something we all share. Our home. It binds us to this blue rock, sets the foundations for all life on Earth, provides food, shelter, warmth and space to play – all while quietly recycling all the elements we need to survive and locking in carbon to secure our future.

At the Soil Association we take every opportunity we can to celebrate the humble soil, and champion the connections it reminds us of. No matter the lives we lead, all routes eventually lead back to the soil. The more people feel connected to it – the nature all around us and the earth beneath our feet – the more we can look after it, and in turn, each other.

Joining together, we can enact lasting change; change that will support our soil, a thriving natural world, and will include and work for everyone.

Best wishes,
Your fellow soil lovers at the Soil Association